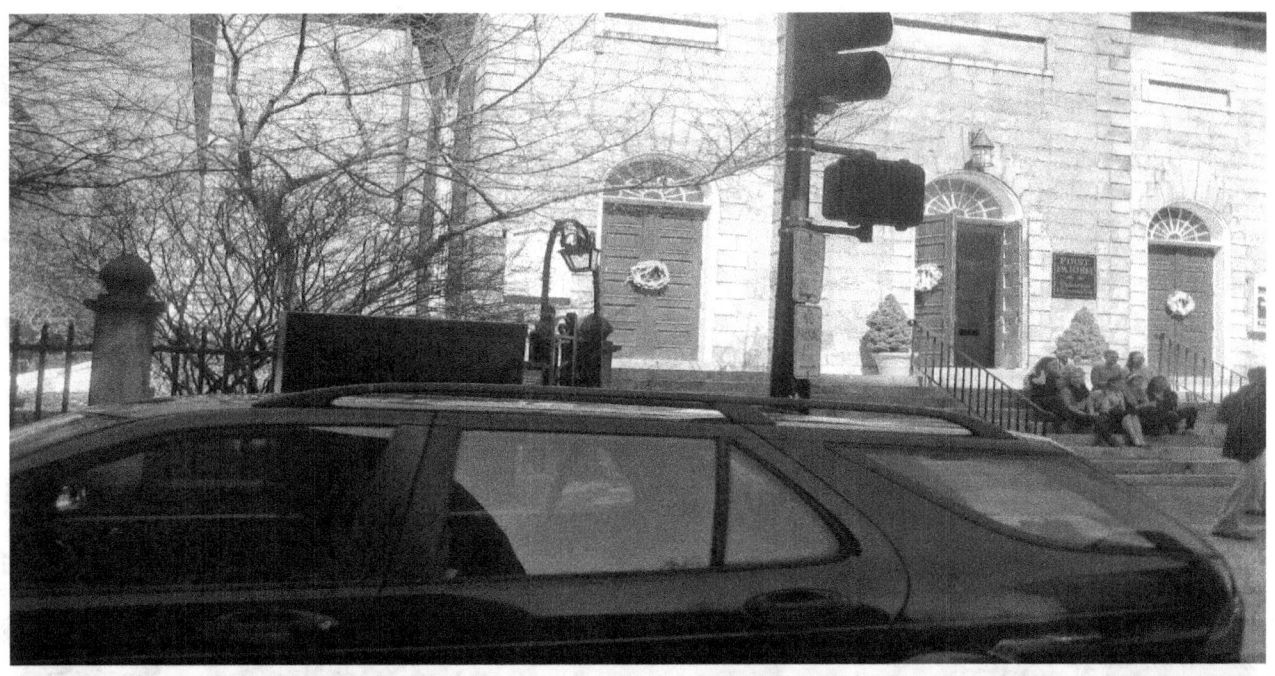

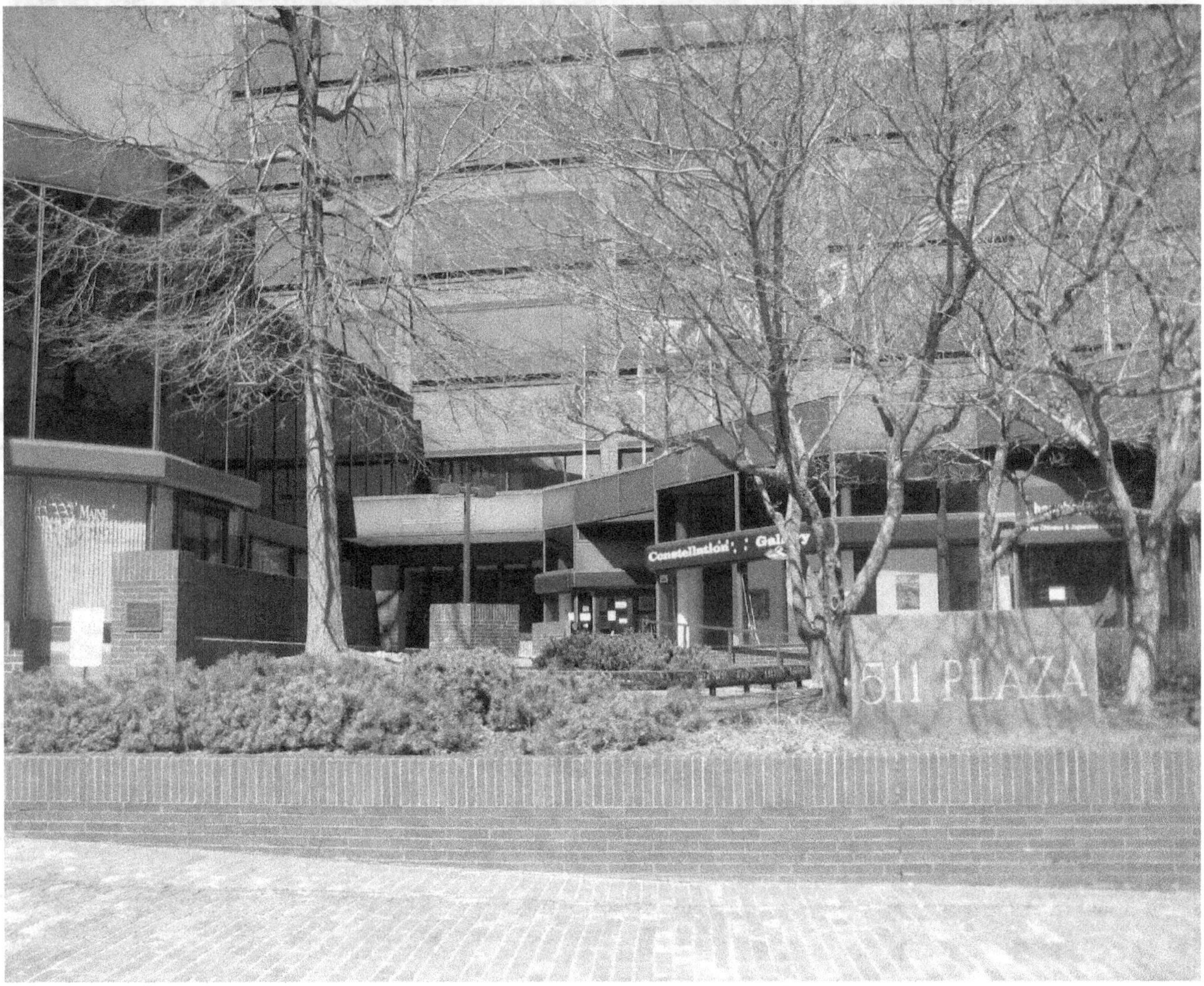
Constellation
511 PLAZA

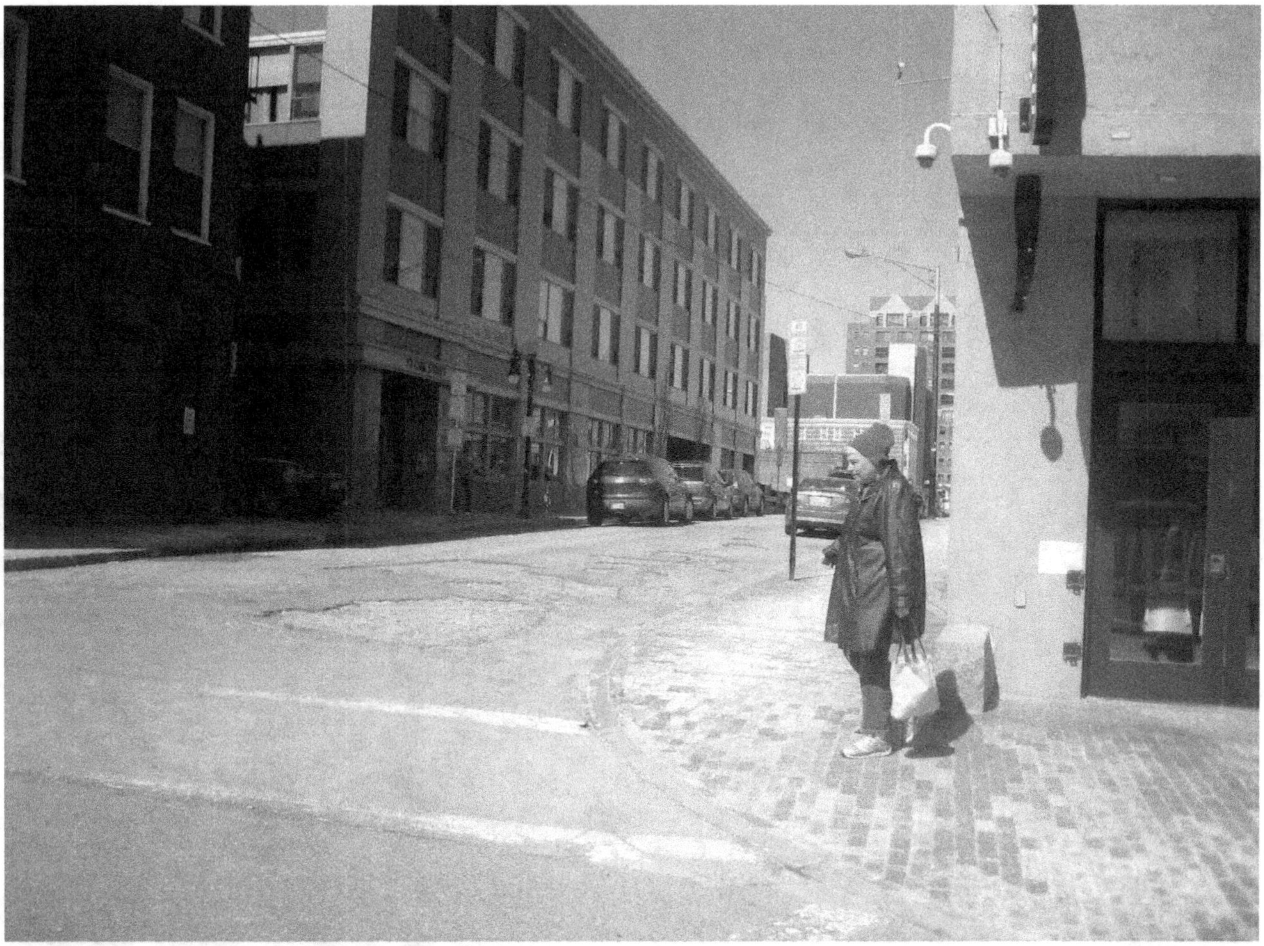

VEHICLE LOADING ZONE
NO PARKING TAXI STAND
YES BOOKS
Prints
PAUL'S
QUALITY FOODS
& A Whole Lot More...

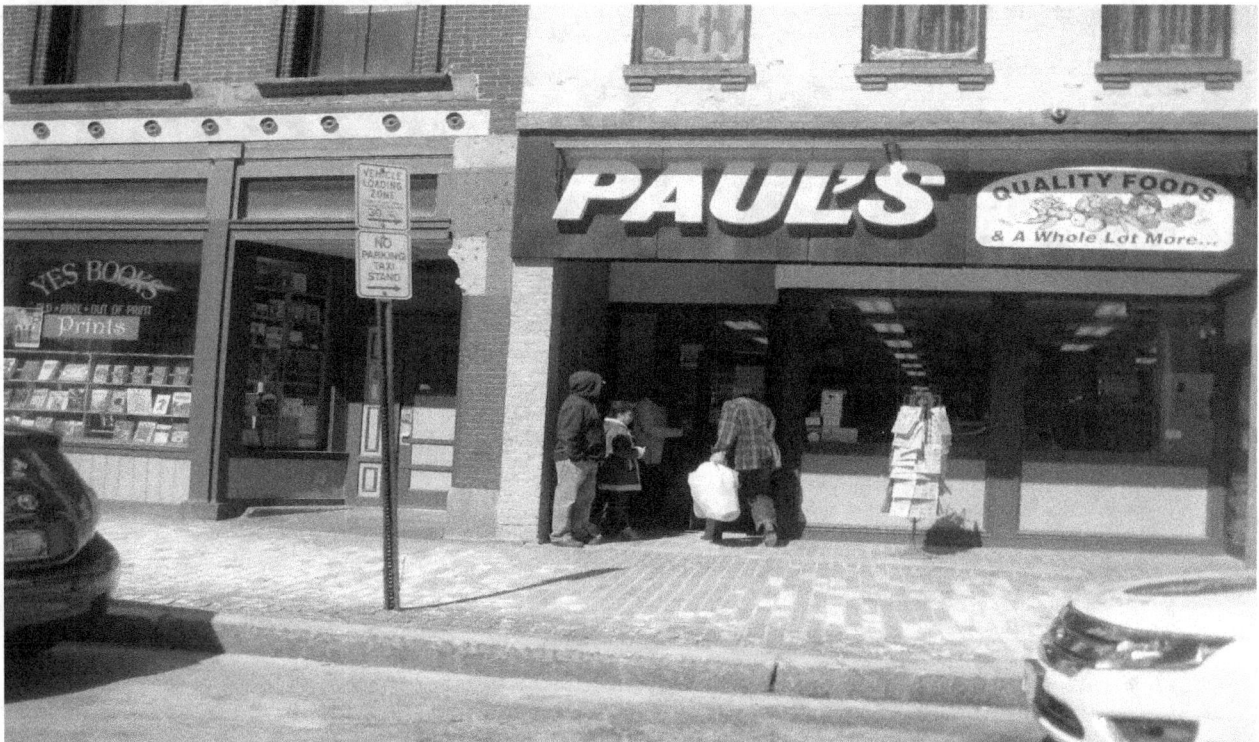

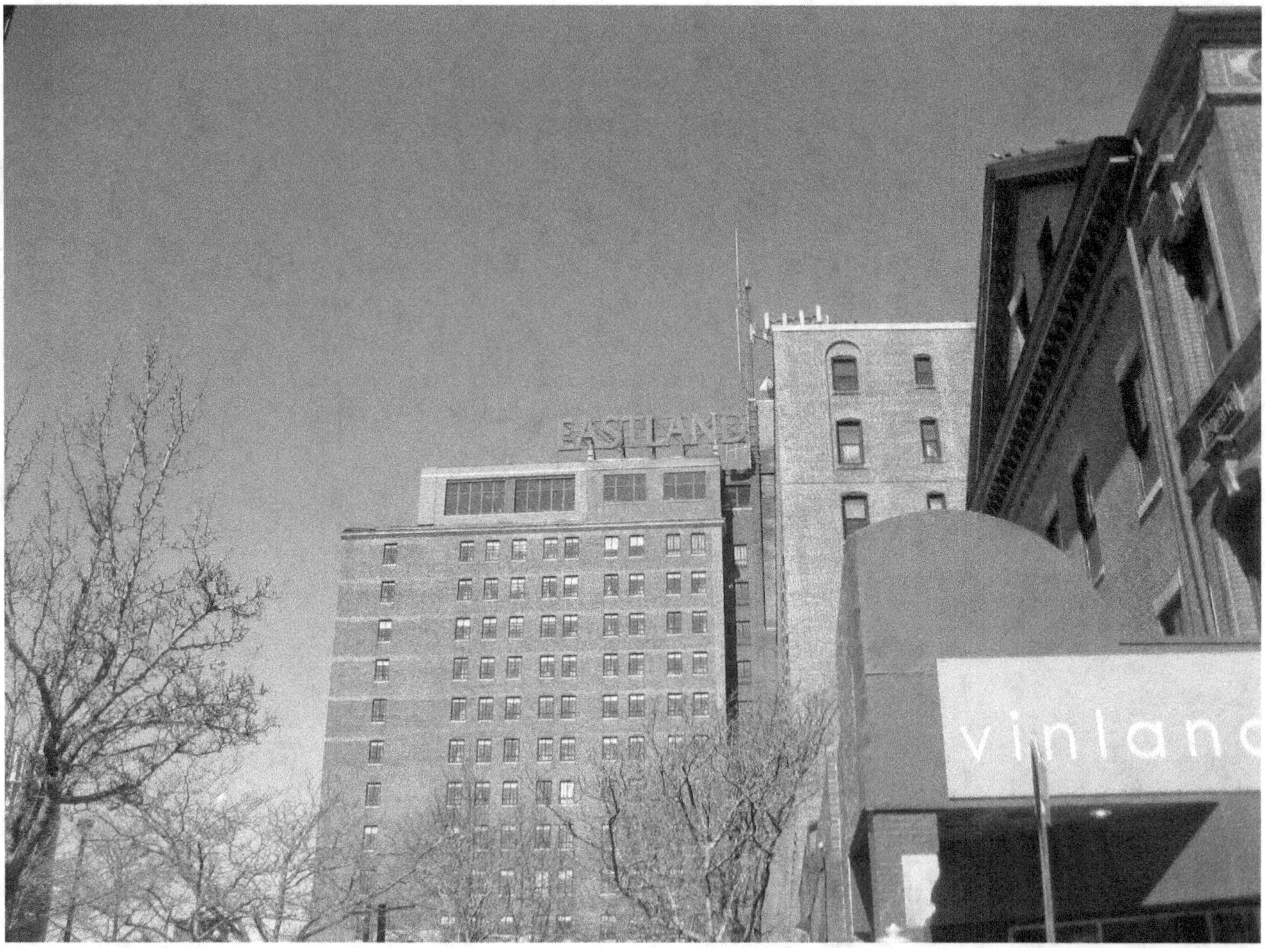
EASTLAND
vinland

THE ART
DEPARTMENT

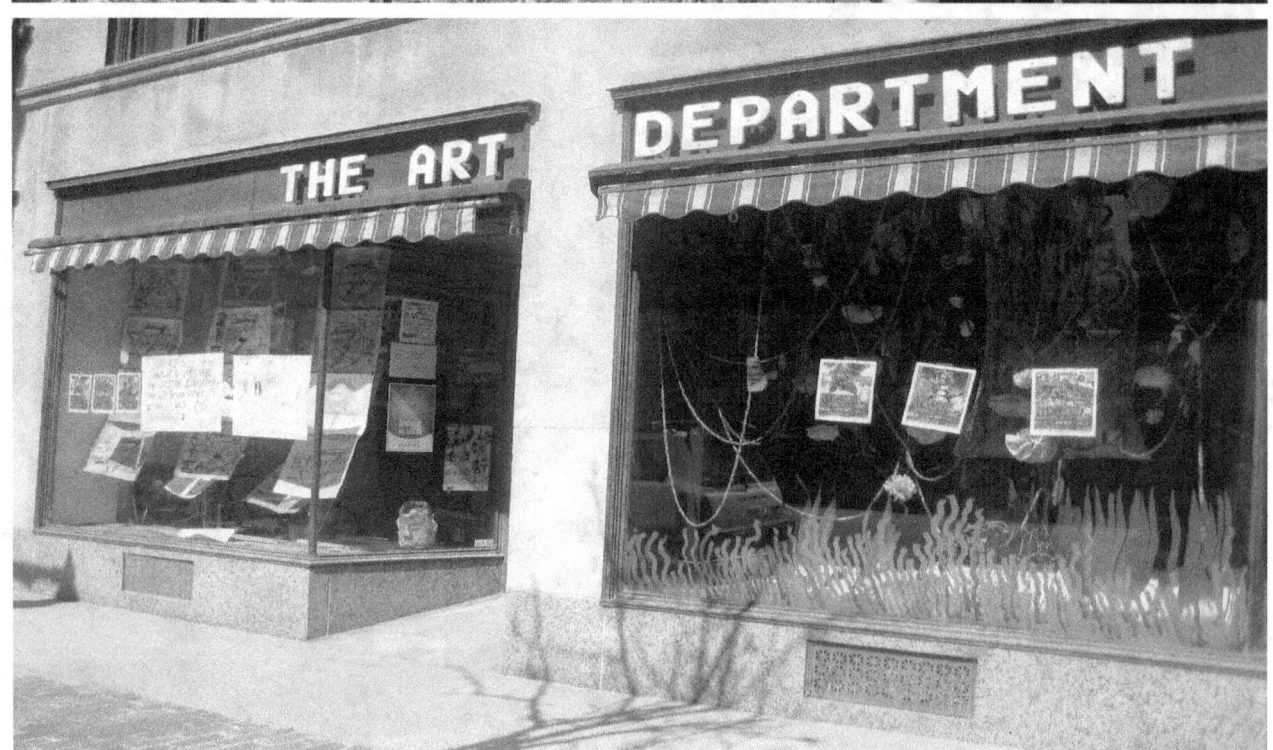

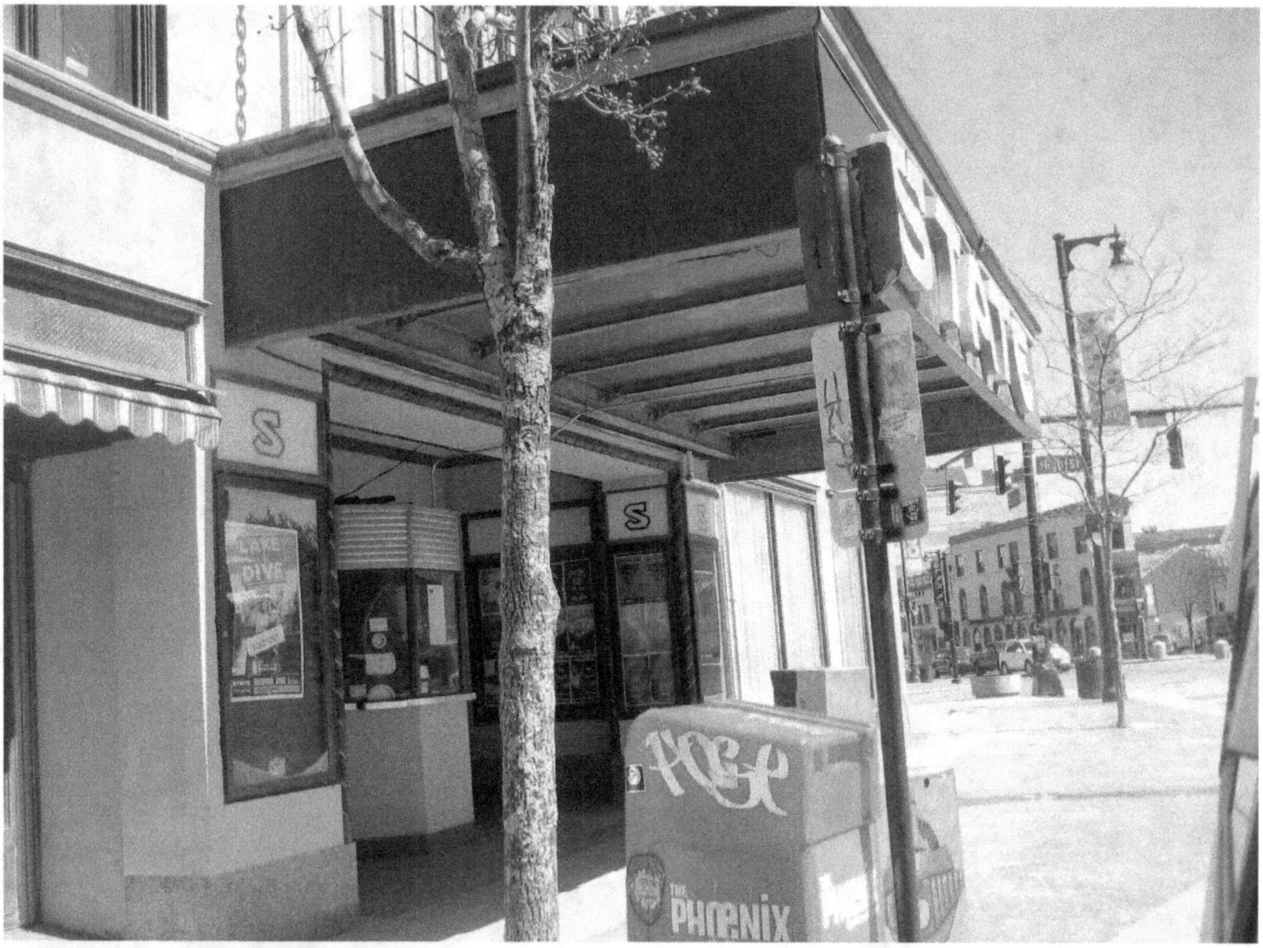
THE
PHŒNIX

UNITED STATES
POSTAL SERVICE
The Portland Sun
Early-Week Edition
FREE
Puppy mill end game?
Oktoberfest event
crosses seasons,
revels in Maine gifts

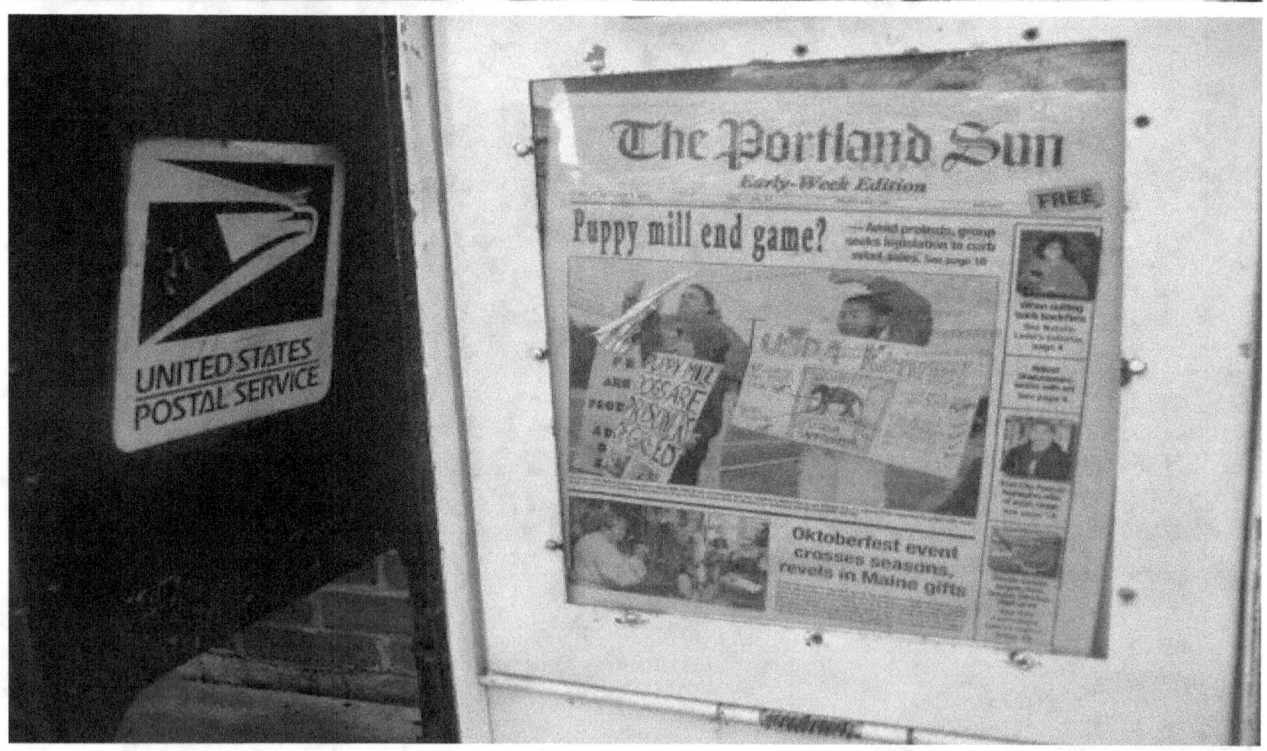

shirleyanitajob.com

# Iceman

**SHIRLEYANITAJOB.COM**

*Banjoe's Hilarity*

## The Peasant James

The Peasant James

---

# Satiated

**BANJOE'S HILARITY**

*shirleyanitajob.com*

## Dr. Tiago Saint Shirley, Esq.

Dr. Tiago Saint Shirley, Esq.

WEEPING
EYES, RENT IN TWAIN, STRAIN TO SEA
WIND WEARY MAGNOLIA TREES AND
WYNTON BURRS REIGNING FREE
SEE ICY SEAS FACE CLIFFS
WHY RELAX MOON EYES
DRIVE WEARY STRAIN WAN
RACE LEFT A NEST A FELT SEA
WE SAW NEW DABS WAX & WAN
BE IT TO THE WHEEL OF FORTUNE
WYNTON WIND AND EYES RIVE TO BE
WEEPING

## Quixotic Quixophasia
~DOPPELGANGER~

JAMES SHIRLEY
"ANITA JOB" BARNES

OXOX

JBS

Speech was given to man to conceal his thoughts.–Charles-Maurice de Talleyrand (~1830)

...

WEEPING

EYES RENT IN TWAIN STRAIN TO SEA

WIND WEARY MAGNOLIA TREES AND

WYNTON BURRS REIGNING FREE

SEE ICY SEAS FACE CLIFFS

WHY RELAX MOON EYES

DRIVE WEARY STRAIN WAN

RACE LEFT A NEST A FELT SEA

WE SAW NEW DAES WAX & WAN

BE IT TO THE WHEEL OF FORTUNE

WYNTON WIND AND EYES RIVE TO BE

WEEPING

EYES

"444"

*shirleyanitajob.com*

Dr. Shirley Anita Job, Esq.

XOXO

jsb

"Heaven
for height,
Earth
for depth
and the heart of kings
is unsearchable."
~ Proverbs

JAMES SHIRLEY BARNES
"ANITA JOB"

SHIRLEYANITAJOB..COM

TIAGO SAINT SHIRLEY

Tiago Saint Shirley

Tiago

WEEPING
, RENT IN TWAIN, STRAIN TC
D W...Y MAGNOLIA TREES
YNT...URRS REIGNING FR
SEE ICY SEAS FACE CLIFFS
WHY RELAX MOON EYES
DRIVE WEARY STRAIN WAN
ACE LEFT A NEST A FELT SE
E SAW NEW DABS WAX & WA
IT TO THE WHEEL OF FORTU
TON WIND AND EYES RIVE T
WEEPING
EYES

QUIXOTIC QUIXOPHASIA        James Shirley "Anita Job" Barnes

WEEPING
EYES, RENT IN TWAIN, STRAIN TO SEA
WIND WEARY MAGNOLIA TREES AND
WYNTON BURRS REIGNING FREE
SEE ICY SEAS FACE CLIFFS
WHY RELAX MOON EYES
DRIVE WEARY STRAIN WAN
RACE LEFT A NEST A FELT SEA
WE SAW NEW DABS WAX & WAN
BE IT TO THE WHEEL OF FORTUNE
WYNTON WIND AND EYES RIVE TO BE
WEEPING

## Quixotic Quixophasia
~DOPPELGÄNGER~

JAMES SHIRLEY
"ANITA JOB" BARNES

# Satiated

creepy crawls spills and plumbs dynamic flushing to sea;
plucked hens click amuck countering cornice cockle-dudes;
synaptical claps placate cystic dens pining nay say sin pangs;
slam saints nit salt in latin sanity saying it to tan city tic slacks;
sublimate supplications surround serene super sonar sounds;
in yesterday, yonkers yammered yarns to yummy mummies;
a neologistic moniker pneumatically abraded sensibilities;
assimilated simplicity pitched charisma against entropy;
latent lament lingers long into waiting moons waning;
daunted vanes vanity vilifies venison during season;
sinisterly claimed core biomes nomenclatures;
acrylic cream flakes mint tulips to sate passion;
every hair is counted by contrary countries;
see icy sea face cliff, why relax moon eye;
limber limbic system intensifies pleasure;
"out damned spot" bloody red summer;
allegoric limericks sharpen story wit;
phobic inflection fuses flagrant fins;
fearsome flares invite vindication;
sully syndicates extrapolate toil;
carbuncle skin reflects boons;
Alone, man ride many miles;

BANJOE'S HILARITY
...dences circulate correlati... Dr. Tiago Saint Shirley, Esq.
...tiple tendencies inspires articulate conspirac...
teeming tenacity tantalizes tendencies to telepathy;
vociferated vernacular veils vanity violently vying;
invisibility invokes a stymied...
intrepid limpid dissipates bray into bloody frays;
lines cognate to limitless m...
colloquial variations consti...
altruistic stipulations crea...
diabolical extremities cloa...
glitterati models quote cli...
scintillating flecks flicker fl...
voracious appetites flaw ch...
clinical literary license evo...
rat race inducts are effica...
as Don Quixote, if ass gets s...
sips of wine while I dine is no...
barnes of existence come in sh...
cairns crane sane paths amids...
raised tables serve statuesque...
concomitant conflation commo...
concordant collegiate limy cro...
snowe balls "alack in unity" de...
ZENGOTE-clamorous monkeys taunt h...
ZYGOTHIX-samson sees delilah babblin...

# BANJOE'S HILARITY
shirleyanitajob.com
Dr. Tiago Saint
Shirley, Esq.

JAMES & THE TECHNICOLOR,
BOOK JACKETS

*shirleyanitajob.com*

Dr. Anita Job, Esq.

May 24, 2013 - Portland, ME, USA

"If it's true what they say about men with big feet, why don't more women marry clowns?"

JSB+RSTP

LOVE

TIAGO SAINT SHIRLEY

Honour et Veritas

Portland, Maine Police
Blotter & Some

AGENT_0PFO

*"I look forward to the day when humans shall have sloughed off the body and become a vortex of thought."* — Harper's Weekly, 1960's

# Twenty-Seven Schizophrenic Scrawls

## Diatribes of a Schizoid

# -JBShirley-

JBShirley

"Some places were better than others to write, but maybe we were not so good in them."

MARLENA'S EIGHTH

MARLENA'S EIGHTH

"56 SHORTS ON MENTAL HEALTH"

-ANONYMOUS-

-Anonymous-

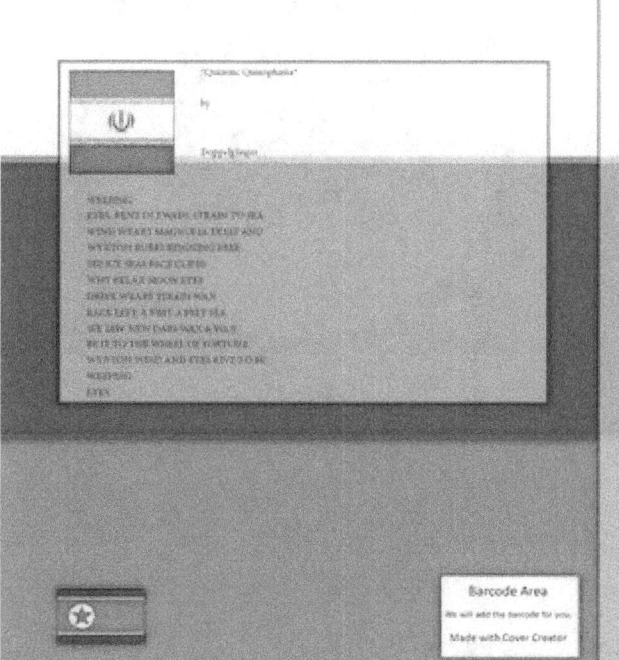

A SHARIA ORIENTS KRONUR

James Shirley "Anita Job" Barnes

A SHARIA ORIENTS KRONUR

*lame jeers shy brains*

James Shirley "Anita Job" Barnes

A Secret Pace

Ninatarajia siku ambapo wanadamu wangepungua mwili na kuwa vortex ya mawazo. ~Harper's

# A Secret Pace
## ~a peace crest~

James Shirley Barnes
"Anita Job"

---

Tasmanian Momster

'liar Liza lies'
-snippet whipper-

A snippet is a brief quotable passage. People who think in snippets are called 'whipper-snippers.'

Women have a greater propensity to hear snippets and deduce from them because they have conversational skills that men don't have and men tend to internalize and think about things differently.

While driving in a car.

Man: Oh! There's that trading firm. I made millions off of them.

Woman: Williams!? What is that!? Williams!? Williams!? What is that!?!

Man: Williams!? What is Williams!? I said millions, whipper-snipper. Where do you get 'williams' from 'millions' talking about that trading firm!?

# Tasmanian Momster

James Barnes
Shirley "Anita Job"

"Hear Visitor"

"Shoot a lion in Zimbabwe and lose a dentist practice in Michigan!"

The Terri Schiavo case was a right-to-die legal case in the United States from 1990 to 2005, involving Theresa Marie "Terri" Schiavo a woman in an irreversible ...

Anagrammatical:

"Terri Shiavo = hear visitor"

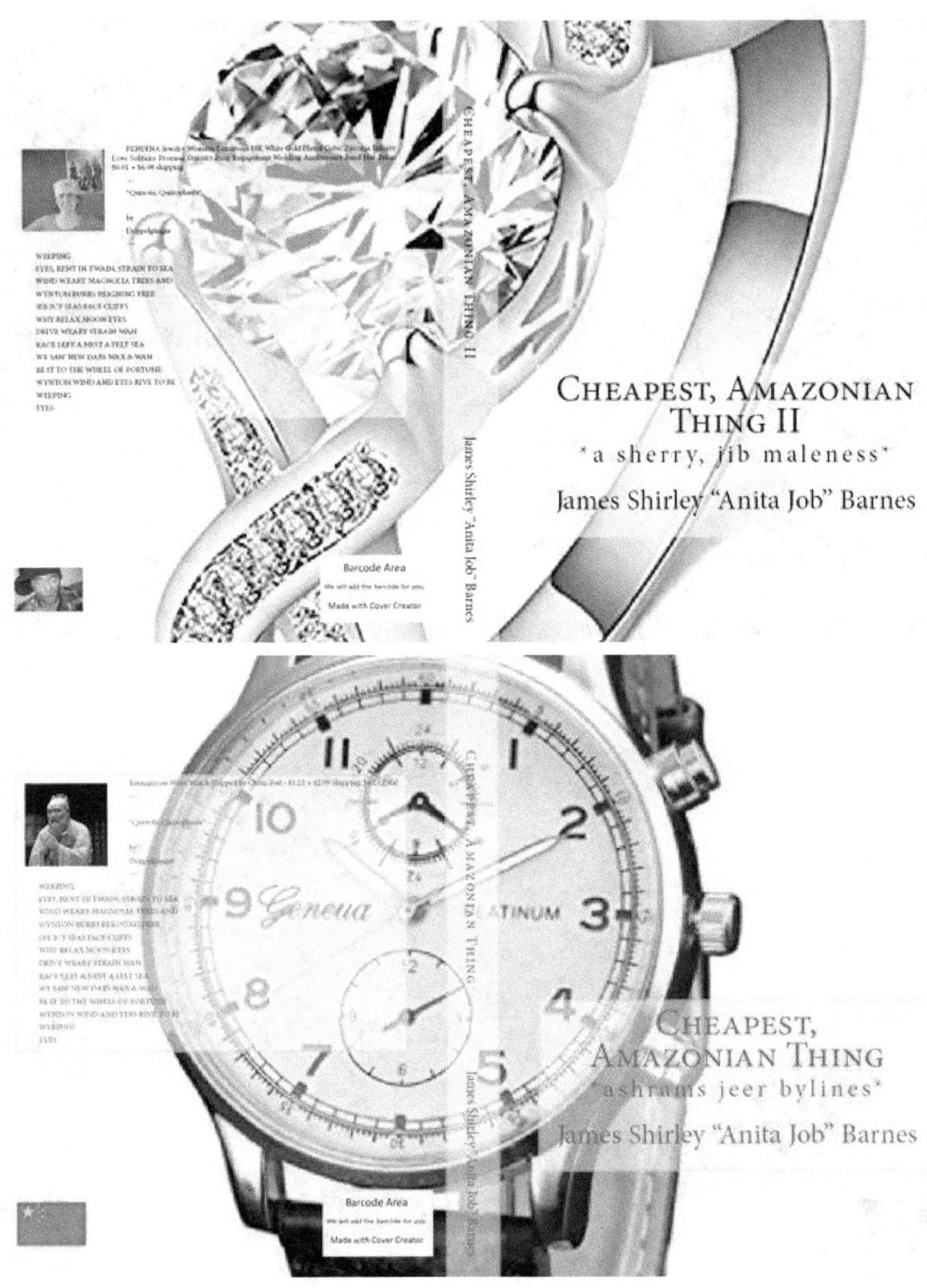

CHEAPEST, AMAZONIAN
THING II
*a sherry, jib maleness*

James Shirley "Anita Job" Barnes

CHEAPEST,
AMAZONIAN THING
*ashrams jeer bylines*

James Shirley "Anita Job" Barnes

49

MAINE CHICKADEE,
AMERICA
'Jersey's her bailsman'

James Shirley "Anita Job" Barnes

A MANIACAL, RICO
QUALIFIER
'Mrs Jersey hens labia'

James Shirley "Anita Job" Barnes

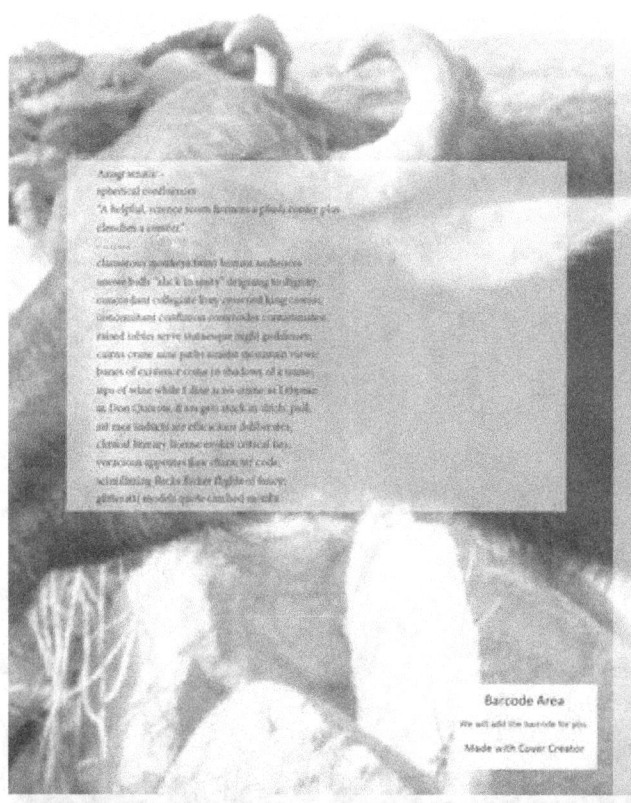

Anagrams:-
spherical confluences

"A helpful, science room features a plush center plus classifies a center"

clamorous monkeys hoist human audiences
secure bells "slick in souts" deigning to dignity,
constant collegiate fray coveted king comes;
concomitant confusion convendes consummates
raised tables serve statuesque night goddesses;
cairns crate acne paths render mountain vistas;
banes of existence come in shadows of a teaser,
sips of wine while I dine as we cruise at Ulysses
as Don Quixote, if we get stuck in ditch, pull,
all men indices are efficacious deliberates;
clerical literary license evokes critical lies;
voracious appetites flee churn in code,
scintillating flecks flicker flights of fancy,
glittery models quote cached mouths

## A Conch's Pencil Refuels
### "spherical confluences" in centrifugal & centripetal forces

### Anita Job

A Conch's Pencil Refuels

Anita Job

---

LOCALES OF MY LIFE :-

LA LUZ, NEW MEXICO
CURRENT CITY
BETHEL, MAINE
MOVED ON OCTOBER 1, 1997
SEATTLE, WASHINGTON
MOVED ON JUNE 1, 1996
BELLINGHAM, WASHINGTON
MOVED ON SEPTEMBER 1, 1994
GABORONE, BOTSWANA
MOVED ON JANUARY 1, 1994
SAN FRANCISCO, CALIFORNIA
MOVED ON AUGUST 1, 1992
ATLANTA, GEORGIA
MOVED ON AUGUST 1, 1991
SOUTHBOROUGH, MASSACHUSETTS
MOVED ON SEPTEMBER 1, 1989
NEW YORK, NEW YORK
MOVED ON AUGUST 1, 1983
BRACKNELL, BERKSHIRE, UK
MOVED ON SEPTEMBER 1, 1981
FREETOWN, SIERRA LEONE
MOVED ON SEPTEMBER 1, 1973
LUBUMBASHI, ZAIRE, (DEMOCRATIC REPUBLIC CONGO) JUNE 1973
HOMETOWN

POSTED BY ~INTERNET TROLL~

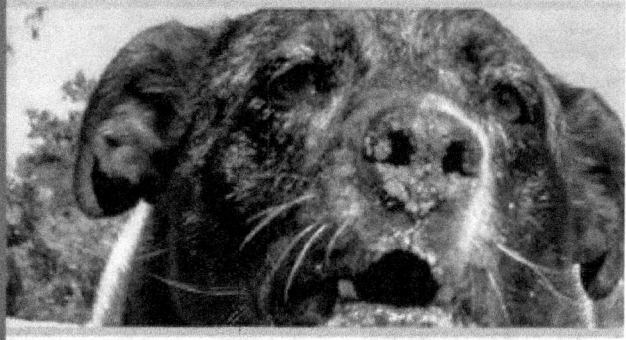

## James & the Technicolor, Book Jackets

### "Shirley Anita Job"

### Mr. James Shirley Barnes

# HOLOGRAPHIC IDENTITIES

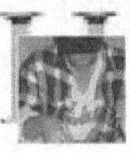

Hidden in the souls and bodies with glaring grey halo canopy,
Gary a nod of my life lined fast past prime slowed birth rate!
Eyes as wide as ales sailing across an empty sea to see
Skies and winds plunged and pale rim below in with cautious
Demure lone lips to wean that pack invaded his salary pies
ever over cries resounding like bleats from slewed sheep to
Why god and why last when paid wrath to an aghast laugh?
Cast out into darkness with weeping and gnashing of teeth!
Are gaile and pink synonymous to altering pure seductions?
Worlds apart draw together in wireless time where at wheel
Distribes at nine eastern nuance her narcissistic intrusions
Orange colors with blue's heads speed to bare grey facades.
Raw, uninhibited emotion was displayed in a crokus to climb.
Pure pains of Paris paset to prosuchetically pray pears perl
Astonished whispers through pipers thin with astonishment
Startles accumulate on shelves shoved in states along acid.
Incipient yet hesitant incoherent activity adheres to jail food flux.
Senses emote meme simply connect sometimes same as all.

## SHERRY'S ABLE JASMINE

anagrammatic

James "Shirley Anita Job" Barnes

---

*James Shirley Barnes*

Goodman:
Knots mirror greyhound funerals
A clear beam to elect a happy fourteenth.
A physician, idle in the eleventh, was in an earthquake.
Weave late ewe with a lent network on a penny and lick tie!
... can music chastise a lewd, black thief to lose a void cross,
He spit in the fifteenth hole to discern dance and being sorry...
Whether thirteenth, eighteenth or thirtieth: shower, lace and a frog.
A dart loops a pigeon toe in apple haven where rail ware vanishes.
A shrewd, twisted pick positions a demonstration which is hale and
A coward motions at crashing planets verses chant magic in a visible
vault.                    -JSB-

James Shirley Barnes

A PHYSICIAN, IDLE IN THE ELEVENTH, WAS IN AN EARTHQUAKE. ANITA "AGENT_0PF0" JOB

PICTURES OF A DULL BABBLER TERMED BEANS ARE: MANGER, SHELTER, A SIXTEENTH OF A CIR- CLE AND OARS. LIEUTENANT: ABASE SEVENTEENTH EGG IN FIFTIETH INK PEN ON EIGHTEEN HEARTH SQUARE, BY DIVERSE COW.

WEEPING
EYES, RENT IN TWAIN, STRAIN TO SEA
WIND WEARY MAGNOLIA TREES AND
WYNTON BURRS REIGNING FREE
SEE ICY SEAS FACE CLIFFS
WHY RELAX MOON EYES
DRIVE WEARY STRAIN WAN
RACE LEFT A NEST A FELT SEA
WE SAW NEW DABS WAX & WAN
BE IT TO THE WHEEL OF FORTUNE
WYNTON WIND AND EYES RIVE TO BE
WEEPING EYES

# A PHYSICIAN, IDLE IN THE ELEVENTH, WAS IN AN EARTHQUAKE.

HE SPIT IN THE FIFTEENTH HOLE TO DISCERN DANCE AND BEING SORRY... WHETHER THIRTEENTH, EIGHTEENTH OR THIRTIETH: SHOWER, LACE AND A FROG.

## ANITA "AGENT_0PF0" JOB

---

DIABOLICAL EXTREMITIES CLOAK SPLIT MINDS ALTRUISTIC STIPULATIONS CREATE QUAGMIRE Anita "Agent_0PF0" Job

-shaikshik charam sremaen alag-alag dimaag; par- opakaaree siddhaanton quagmirais banaate hain; as- titv ka jhukaav ek naam kee chhaaya mein aata hai; jab main bhojan karata hoon to sharaab kee soore koee aparaadh nahin hai kyonki main kavita-

coagulate correspondences circulate correlated words;
a cad ass sits, splits and planks dynamos flushing to sea;
creepy crawls crammed creamy crimson cones in collision;
plucked hens clock amuck countering cornice cockle-dudes;
synaptical claps placate cystic clans pining nay say sin pangs;
slain saints nit salt in latin sanity saving it to tan city tic slacks;
sublimate supplications surround serene super sonar sounds;
in yesterday, yonkers yammered yarns to yummy mummies;
a neologistic moniker pneumatically abraded sensibilities;

### DIABOLICAL EXTREMITIES CLOAK SPLIT MINDS ALTRUISTIC STIPULATIONS CREATE QUAGMIRE

banes of existence come in shadows of a name;
sips of wine while I dine is no crime as I rhyme

## Anita "Agent_0PF0" Job

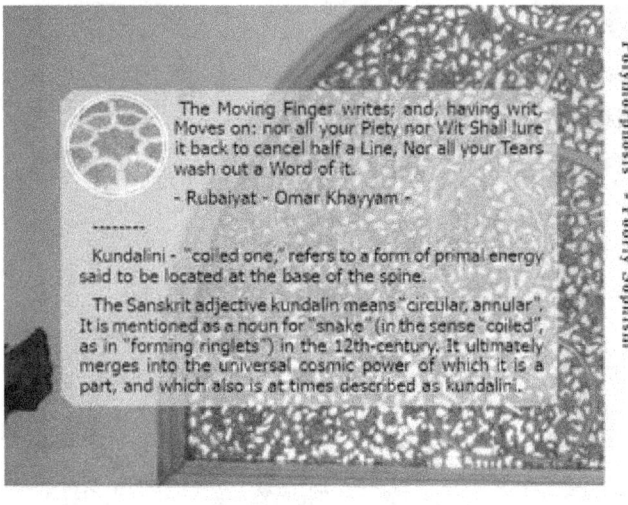

The Moving Finger writes; and, having writ, Moves on: nor all your Piety nor Wit Shall lure it back to cancel half a Line, Nor all your Tears wash out a Word of it.

- Rubaiyat - Omar Khayyam -

--------

Kundalini - "coiled one," refers to a form of primal energy said to be located at the base of the spine.

The Sanskrit adjective kundalin means "circular, annular". It is mentioned as a noun for "snake" (in the sense "coiled", as in "forming ringlets") in the 12th-century. It ultimately merges into the universal cosmic power of which it is a part, and which also is at times described as kundalini.

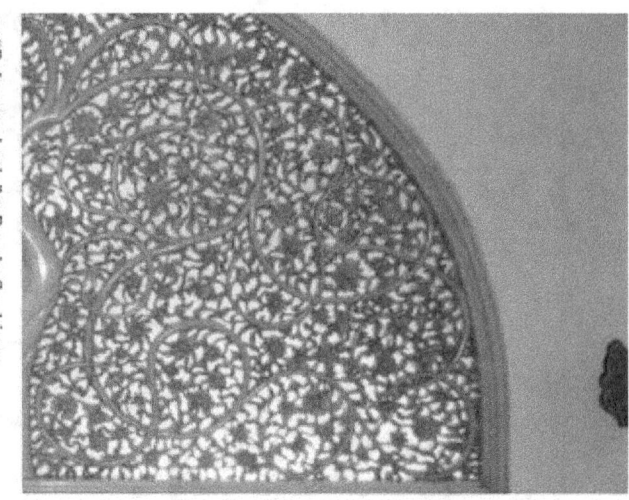

## "Polymorphosis" - Poorly Sophism

Polymorph is a mage spell that transforms the enemy into a critter, removing it from combat.

# Anita "Agent_0PF0" Job

**"Polymorphosis" - Poorly Sophism**

**Anita "Agent_0PF0" Job**

MONKS SORT A RIFLER URN; INFORM A SNORTER'S LURK.
...A Miser's Forlorn-Trunk Mirrors A Felon's Trunk...
Anita "Agent_0PF0" Job

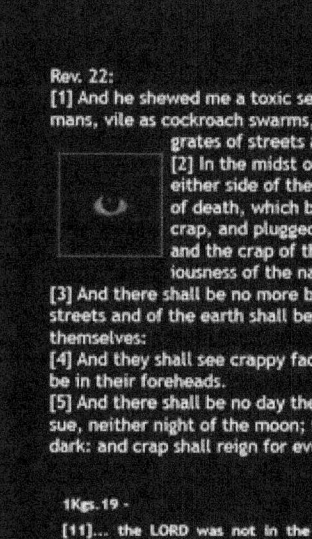

gnat hell.

Knots Mirror Greyhound Funerals

Anita "Agent_0PF0" Job

## Knots Mirror Greyhound Funerals

A coward motions at crashing planets verses chant magic in a visible vault.

Anita "Agent_0PF0" Job

---

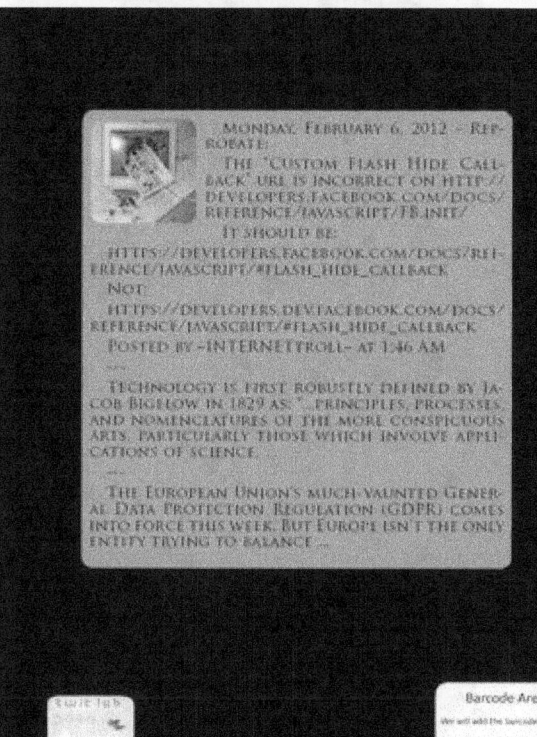

MINIMISE DATA, TIMID AMNESIA. DAINTIES MAIM AIMED ANIMISM. I MISTED MANIA.

ANITA "AGENT_0PF0" JOB

### gnat hell.

INDIA SAM MIME A MIDI MISNAME.
I MISNAME MAID A MAD. MISE.
MINI. MEDIA ANIMISM.

## ANITA "AGENT_0PF0" JOB

*"What are some psychological ramifications and descriptive words of the described scenario?"*

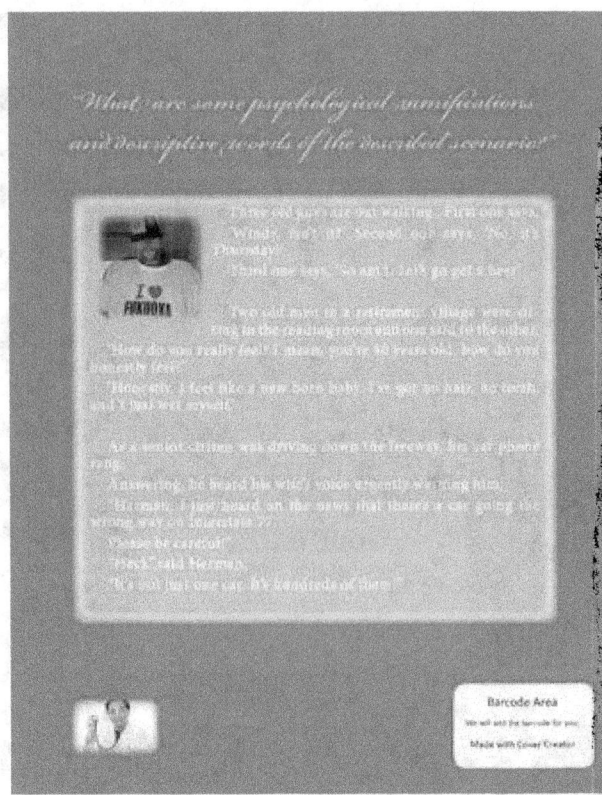

ANITA "AGENT_OPFO" JOB

"BE A GOOD SAVAGE!"

BE A GOOD SAVAGE!

---

Was-it-the-Media-Animism?

"Results for your search for 'Media Animism':"

"... forums is where I play "Infinite Chess" using lexicons as my pieces. Hence: "Media Animism," or, "Media Animist." ex.: I could stand in the middle of a South of France, nudist beach and shoot somebody and sell the photos to Playboy or Playgirl; where "Playboy" is not, "Playboy. ...", etc., and it gets them all confused every time. Playboy Playboy difference lies in a capital I as opposed to a lower case L. So many things that I have uncovered since HTY Fo, then word fo and now opfo... lerb much on opfo and fos.

Knight's variation from even to odd in game, set control differences and parabolas of board matrices, but: "Media Animism" is here to stay. ...

"I could stand in the middle of 5th Ave and shoot ..."

- POTUS Candidate, 23 January, 2016, IA

Doctor, Dr. Doctor, Dr. FBIMan, Dr. Secret Service, Dr. Police Officer, Dr. Etc.

"Everybody is a Doctor"

Anita "Agent_OPFO" Job

"Évolution du prix de 10 produits de base entre 2001 et 2011: Les Français se plaignent de l'euro. Il aurait permis aux commerçants d'augmenter les prix. Ceux-ci disent que c'est la faute au surcoût des charges sociales et des matières premières. Une enquête parue dans le magazine Valeurs Actuelles."

"In a large bowl, combine flour, sugar, baking powder, baking soda, and salt. In a separate bowl, beat together buttermilk, milk, eggs and melted butter. ... Heat a lightly oiled griddle or frying pan over medium high heat. ... Pour the wet mixture into the dry mixture, using a wooden spoon or fork to blend."

"Instructions: Use around 1 shot glass full of ingredients per 2 cups of water. Transfer ingredients to t-sac or t-ball. Place in cup. Add boiling water. Steeping time depends on desired intensity of flavor."

mainenutrition.blogspot.com

Anita "Agent_0PF0" Job

**mainenutrition.blogspot.com**

"Yes! I'd love a sandwich & a bier. ..."

## Anita "Agent_0PF0" Job

"All dogs do go to Heaven." — Pope Francis

"Since ancient times, the image of Romulus and Remus being suckled by a she-wolf has been a symbol of the city of Rome."

"As a dog returneth to vomit, so doth a fool to folly."

"Everything I know I learned from dogs."

"A dog is the only thing on earth that loves you more than you love yourself. Money can buy you a fine dog, but only love can make him wag his tail. The dog is the perfect portrait subject. Animals have come to mean so much in our lives. A dog will teach you unconditional love."

"Cat will mew, dog will have his day!"

IT IS IMPORTANT NOT TO OVERLOOK THE LOVE OF AN ANIMAL

"No matter the animal, if shown love, the animal will love back."

Anita Job
"Agent_0PF0"

"I don't know whether to get all those virgins." — Ed Jones

"Don't judge a book by its cover!"

A snippet is a brief quotable passage. People who think in snippets are called 'whipper-snippets.'

Women have a greater propensity to hear snippets and deduce from them because they have conversational skills that men don't have and men tend to internalize and think about things differently.

While driving in a car ...

Man: Oh! There's that trading firm. I made millions off of them.
Woman: Williams? What is that!? Williams!? Williams!? What is that!?
Man: Williams!? What is Williams!? I said millions, 'whipper-snipper'. Where do you get 'williams' from 'millions' talking about that trading firm!?

Barcode Area
We will add the barcode for you
Made with Cover Creator

"The Peasant Jam is Virgin"

Anita Job
"Agent_OPFO"

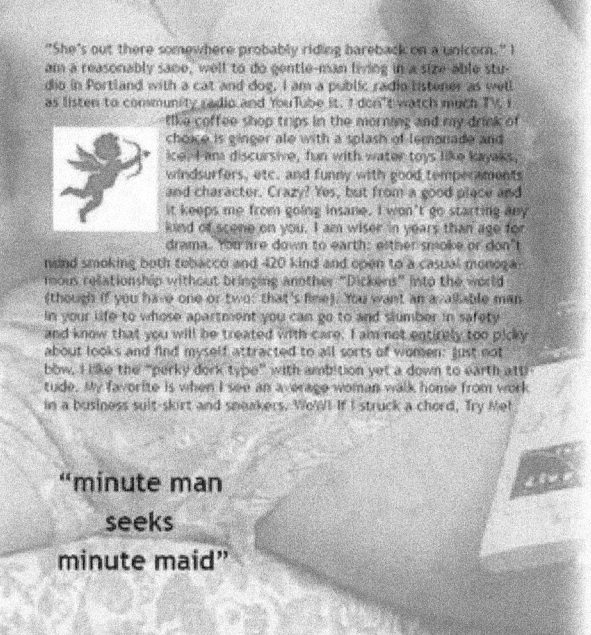

"She's out there somewhere probably riding bareback on a unicorn." I am a reasonably sane, well to do gentle-man living in a size able studio in Portland with a cat and dog. I am a public radio listener as well as listen to community radio and YouTube it. I don't watch much TV. I like coffee shop trips in the morning and my drink of choice is ginger ale with a splash of lemonade and ice. I am discursive, fun with water toys like kayaks, windsurfers, etc. and funny with good temperaments and character. Crazy? Yes, but from a good place and it keeps me from going insane. I won't go starting any kind of scene on you. I am wiser in years than age for drama. You are down to earth: either smoke or don't mind smoking both tobacco and 420 kind and open to a casual monogamous relationship without bringing another "Dickens" into the world (though if you have one or two: that's fine). You want an available man in your life to whose apartment you can go to and slumber in safety and know that you will be treated with care. I am not entirely too picky about looks and find myself attracted to all sorts of women: just not bbw. I like the "perky dork type" with ambition yet a down to earth attitude. My favorite is when I see an average woman walk home from work in a business suit-skirt and sneakers. WoW! If I struck a chord, Try Me!

"minute man

seeks

minute maid"

Barcode Area
We will add the barcode for you
Made with Cover Creator

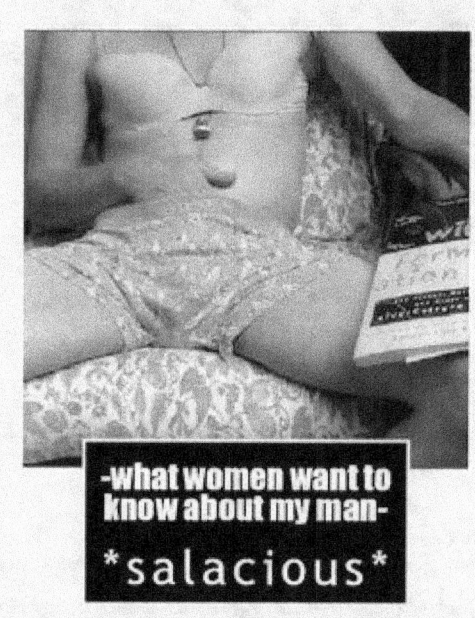

-what women want to know about my man-

-what women want to
know about my man-
*salacious*

Anita "Agent_OPFO" Job

*"'I could stand in the middle of 5th Avenue and shoot somebody. ...' and sell the photos to 'Person of the Year!'"* 23 January, 2016, IA

"Don't judge a book by its cover!"

---------

Meghan Markle borrowed Queen Mary's bandeau tiara from Queen Elizabeth for the Royal Wedding. Here's everything you need to know about the gorgeous diamond piece. ...

May 16, 2015 - The Queen Mary may have retired from her oceangoing days, but she ... Pro tip: The Fourth of July fireworks show is a hot ticket. ... Designer names like Prada, Valentino and Cartier are a dime a-diamond-encrusted dozen here. ....

Nov 20, 2013 - Queen Mary 2 Transatlantic Crossing Featuring James Taylor ... European tour aboard QUEEN MARY 2 on the August 27, 2014 Transatlantic ... albums and earning 40 Gold, Platinum, Multi-Platinum and Diamond awards, ...

---------

"James Taylor!?" gaads. I'm glad that I live in my "dump!" Not much to worry about here. ... xoxo

Anita "Agent_0PF0" Job

< *DonaId_Trurnp* >

"Stormy out. ... better wear a rain coat!"

Anita "Agent_0PF0" Job

---

*"He's our king."*
*"How do you know that?"*
*"He hasn't got shit all over him!"*

"Scatological Eschatology:"
Eschatology, a branch of theology that studies the end times, often attracts writers who, like scientists, seek to prove, quantify and make predictions. These students sift the Bible for metaphor and symbol, searching for meaning in what are often puzzling passages in scripture. It helps to remember that a doomsday event has seemed reasonable for centuries, given the chaos inflicted by natural disasters, pandemics and perfervid world leaders.

- "Quixophasia," Monday, October 17, 2011

---------

Eschatological Scatology is the seventh full-length studio album by Gnaw Their Tongues, independently released on June 6, 2012.

gnat hell.

Anita "Agent_0PF0" Job

"SCATOLOGICAL ESCHATOLOGY"

ANITA "AGENT_0PF0" JOB

*"Scatological Eschatology"*

"Today is Saturday, I'm going to do as 'Don Quixote' does and if my ass gets stuck in a ditch, I'm going to pull it out."

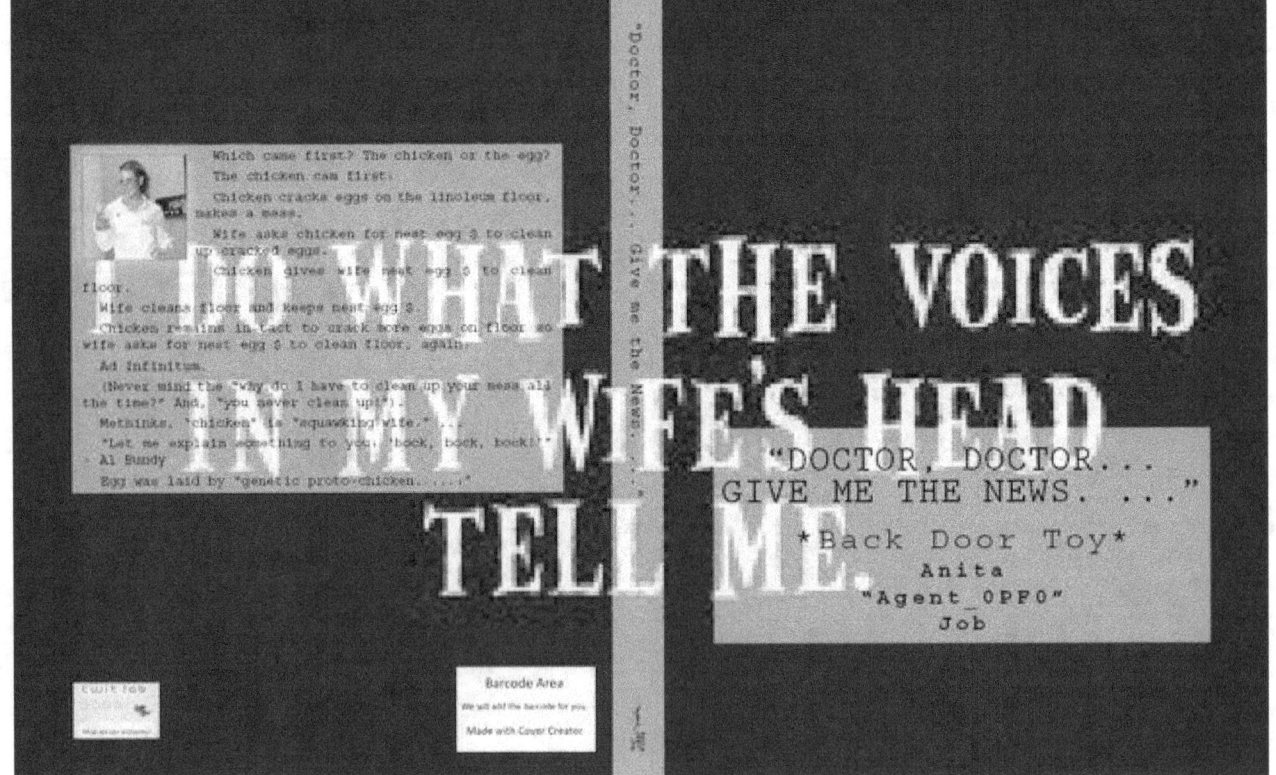

 I was telecommuting from my apartment to New Jersey re-cruiting lawyers for a 450/hr job when a lawyer says: "why would I do that? I make 700/hr."

I replied "good for you. I make 10/hr calling you."

He hung up.

--------

Prison smoke traced to inmate cooking in toilet: talk about noxious stimuli: he'd give for homemade pie! I tell you no lie, my my my: what he'd give for some rye! Almost makes you want to cry: sleeping so close and nearby- a stink pile and a fry pan- makes for a great big sigh!

ANITA "AGENT_OPF0" JOB

"BANANA HAMMOCK"

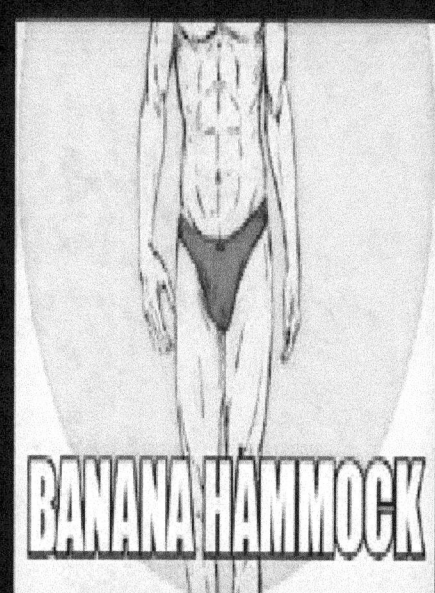

BANANA HAMMOCK

Anita "Agent_OPF0" Job

"Banana Hammock"

-a thong for men-

FENDINA Jewelry Womens Luxurious 18K White Gold Plated Cubic Zirconia Infinity Love Solitaire Promise Eternity Ring Engagement Wedding Anniversary Band Her

Princely Price $0.01 + $6.98 Shipping

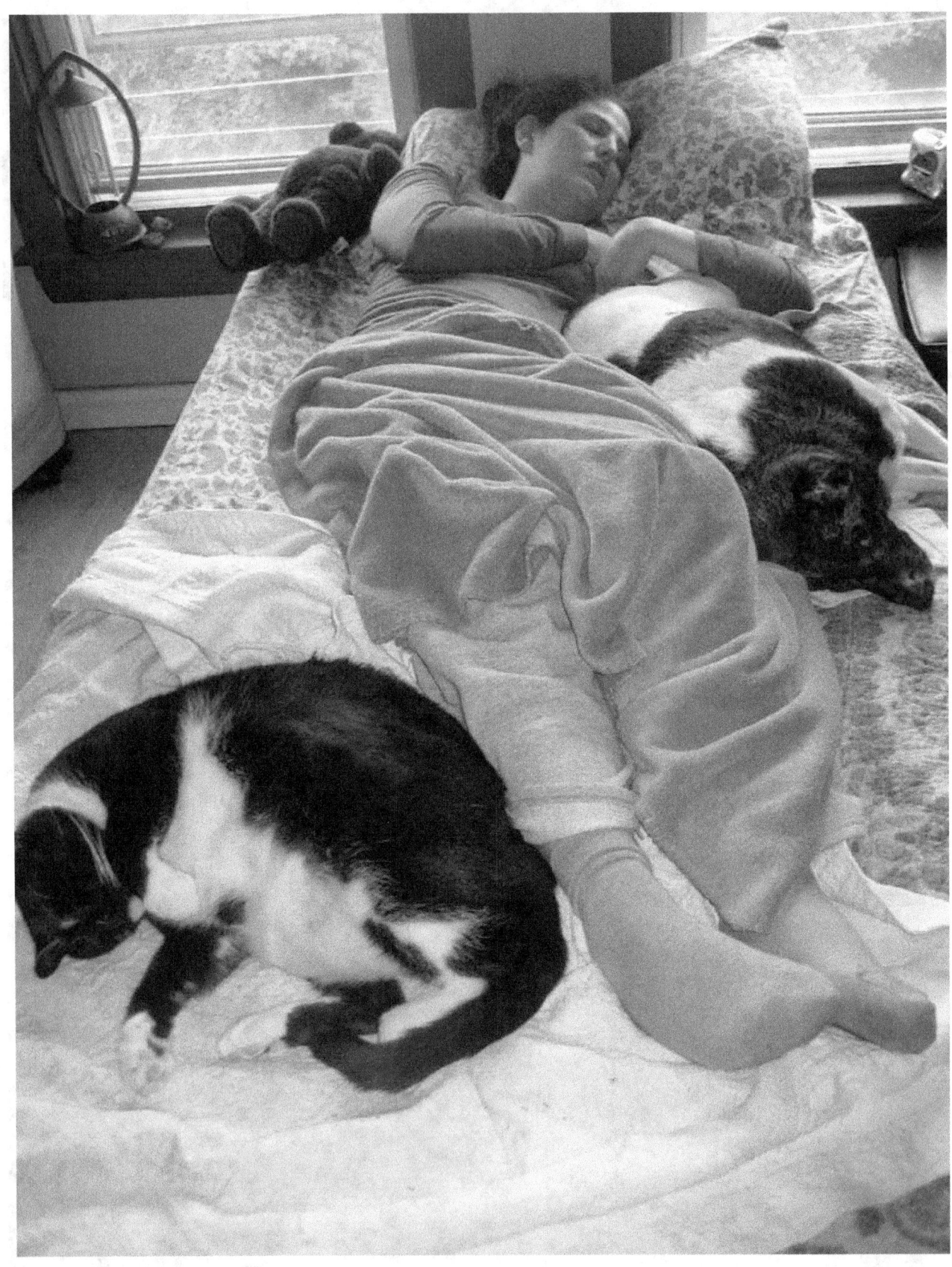

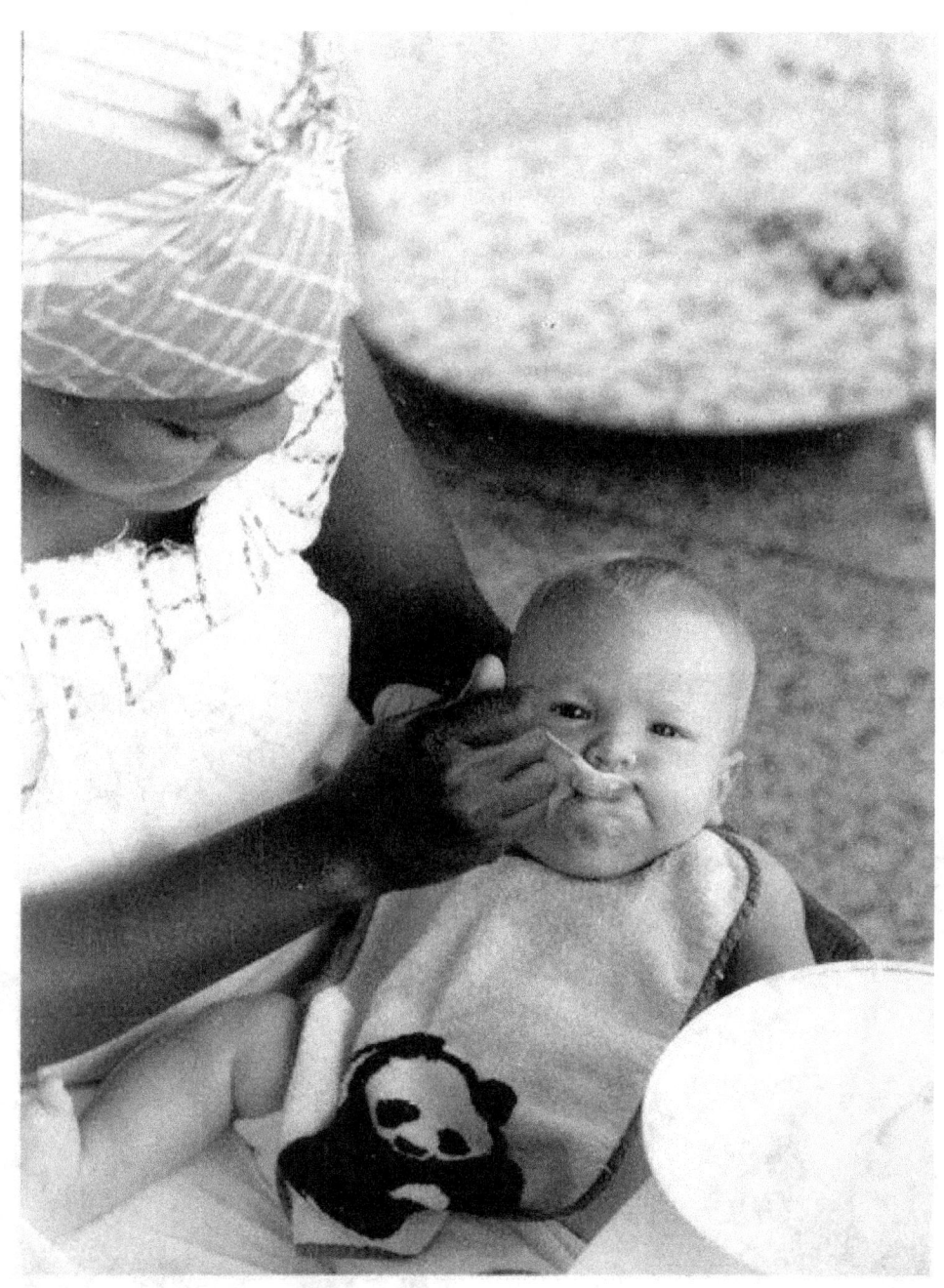

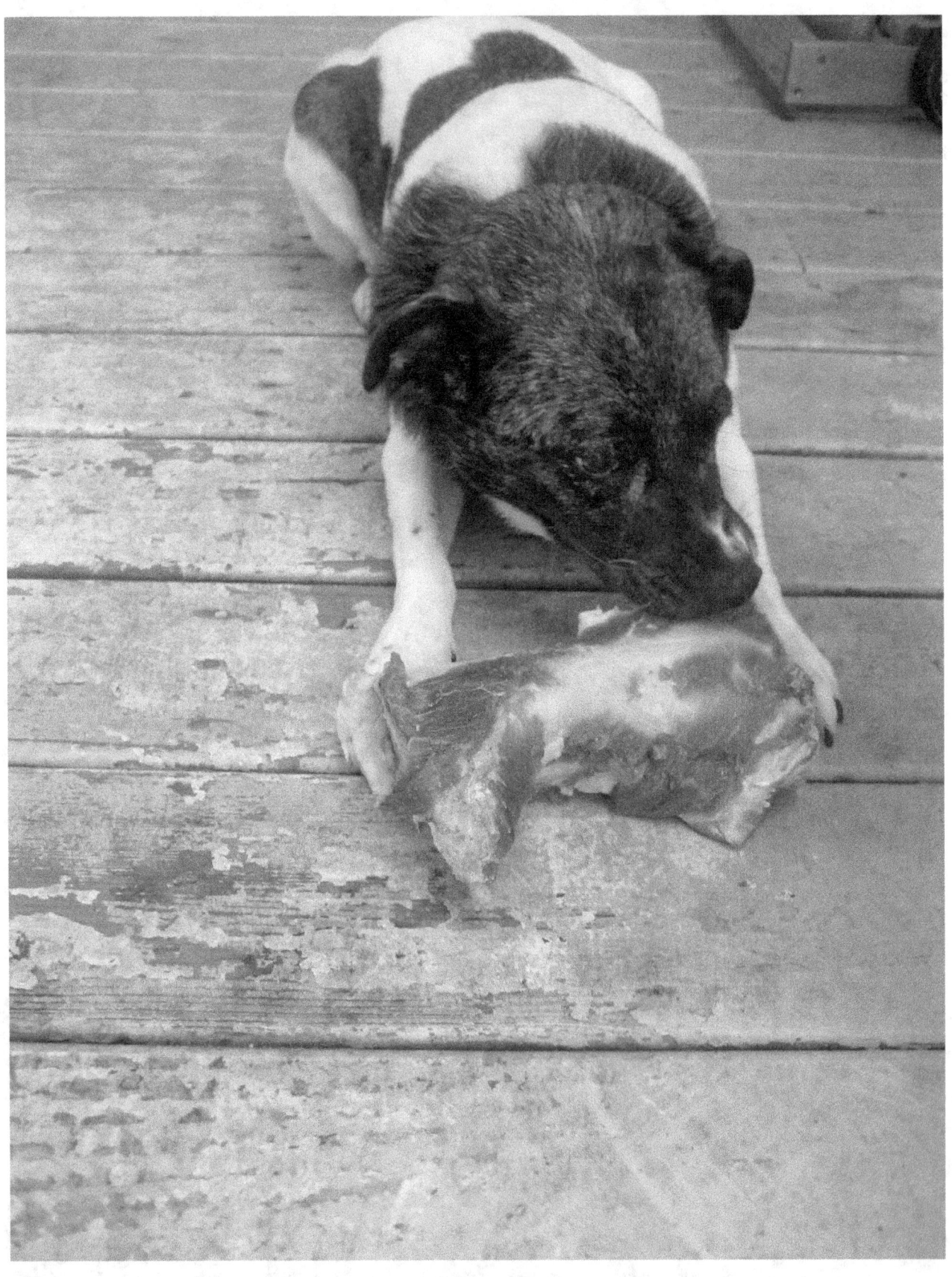

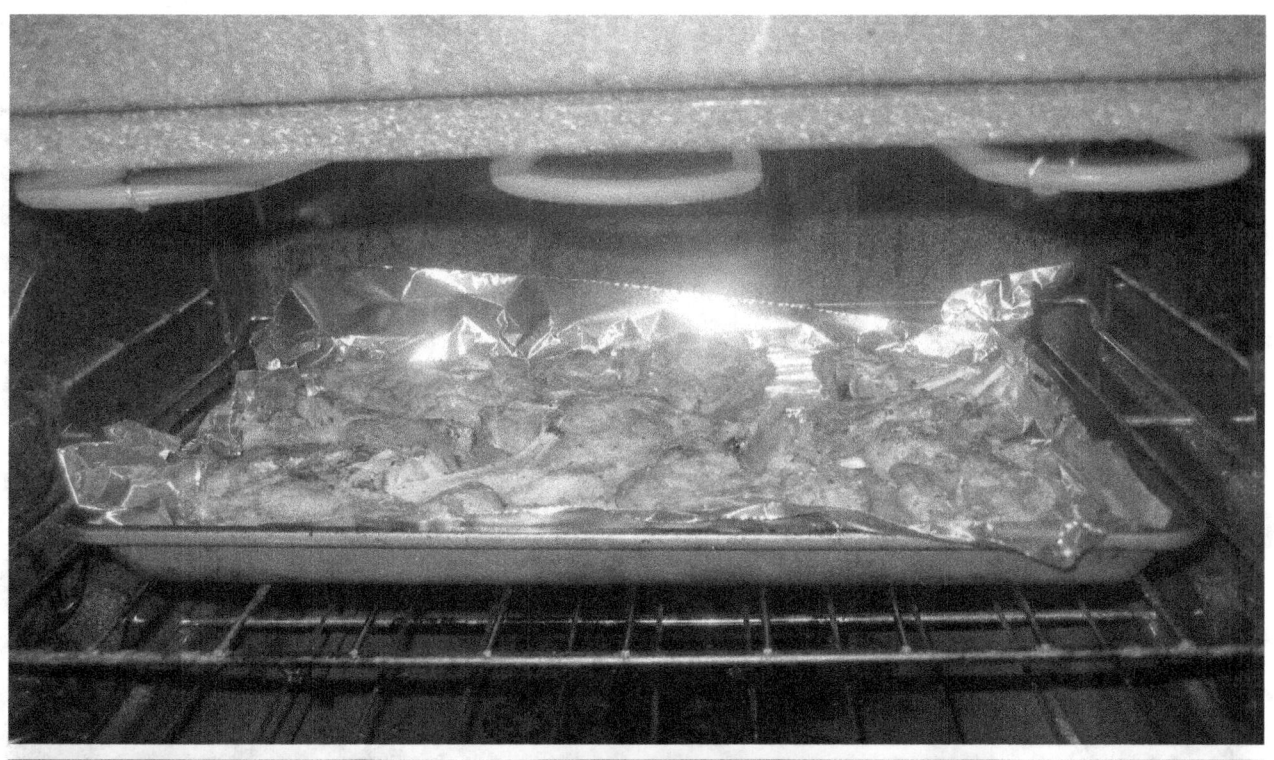

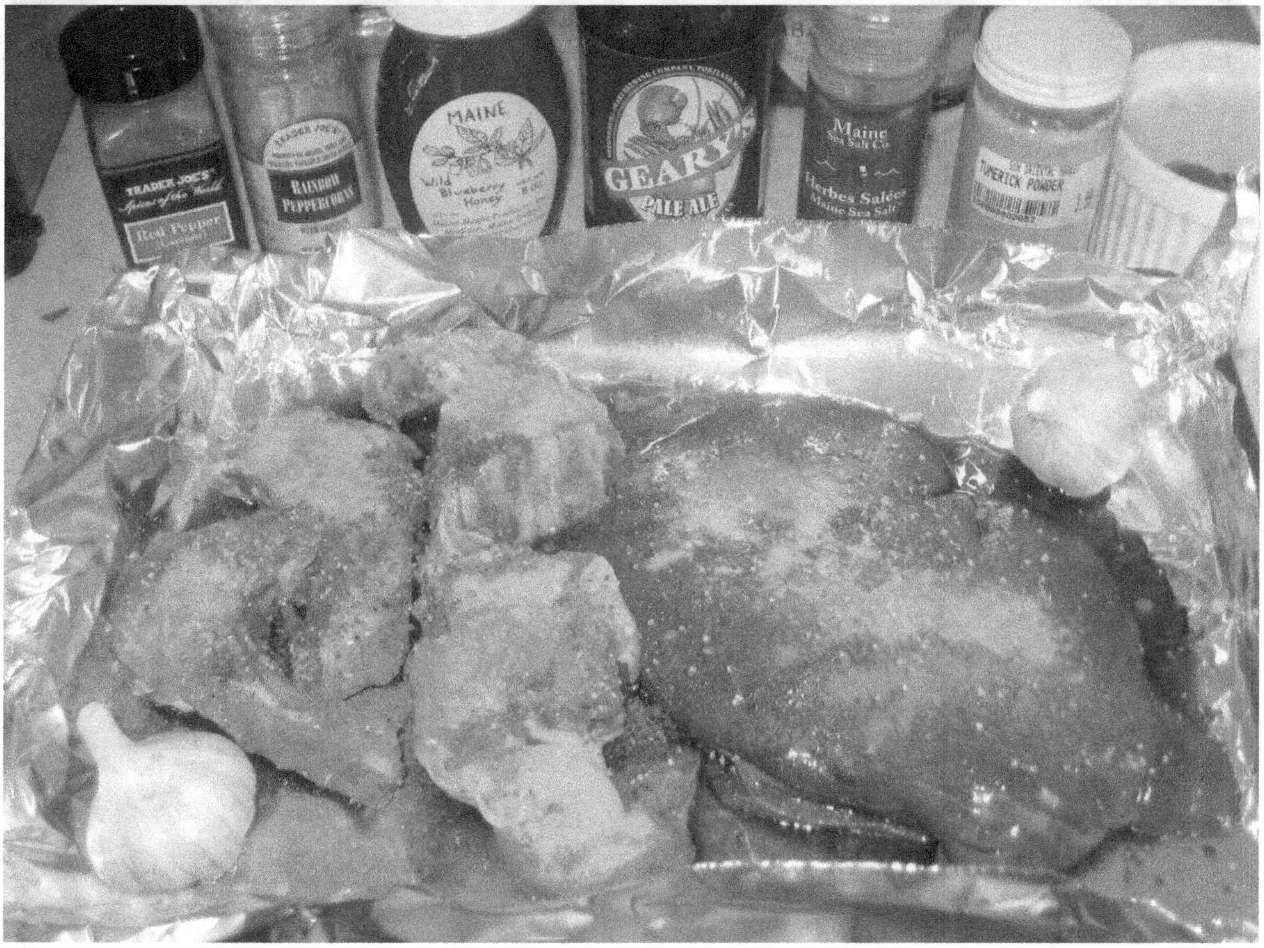
TRADER JOE'S
Spices of the World
Red Pepper
RAINBOW PEPPERCORNS
MAINE
Wild Blueberry Honey
GEARY'S
PALE ALE
Maine Sea Salt Co.
Herbes Salées
Maine Sea Salt
TUMERICK POWDER

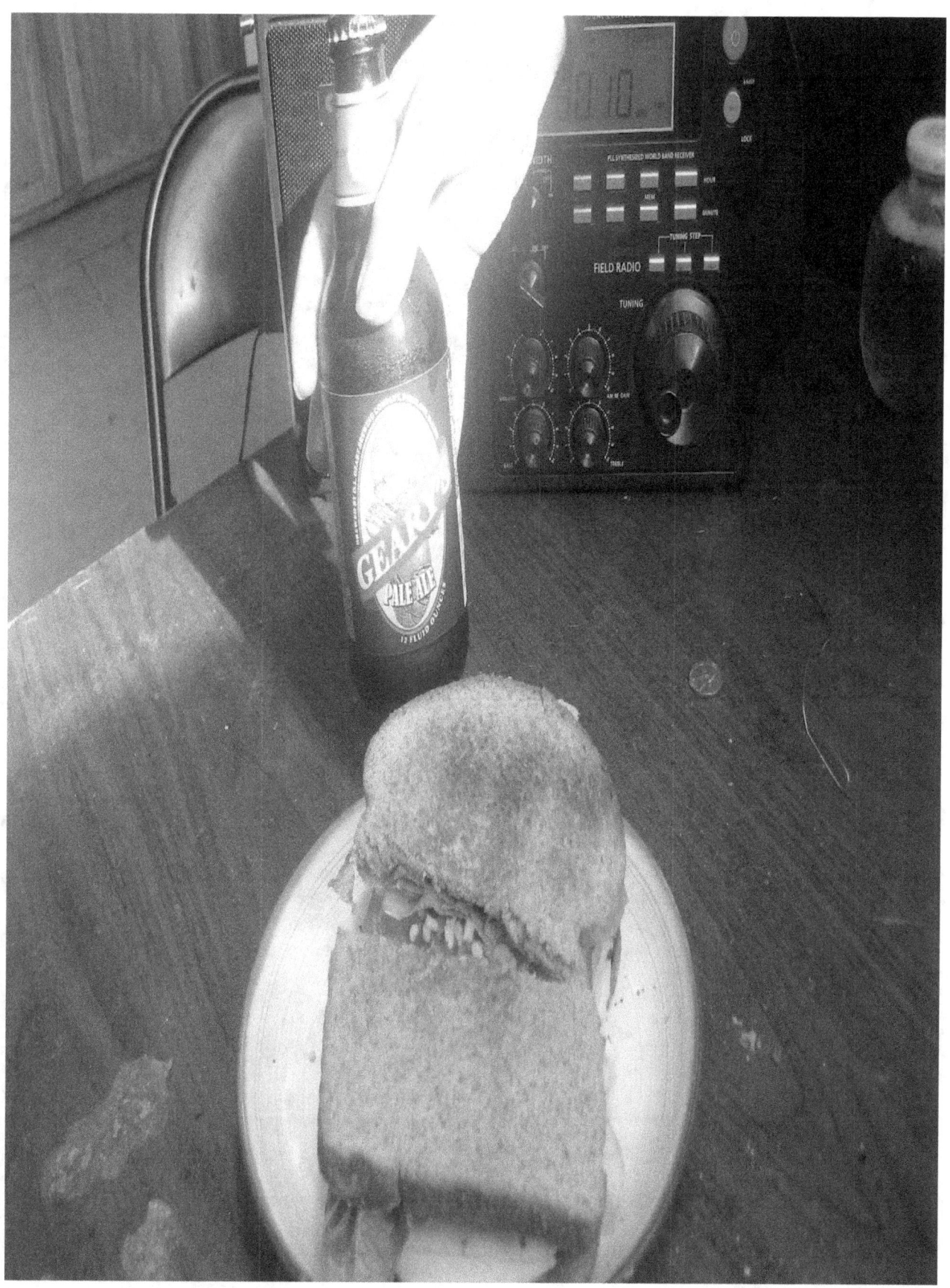

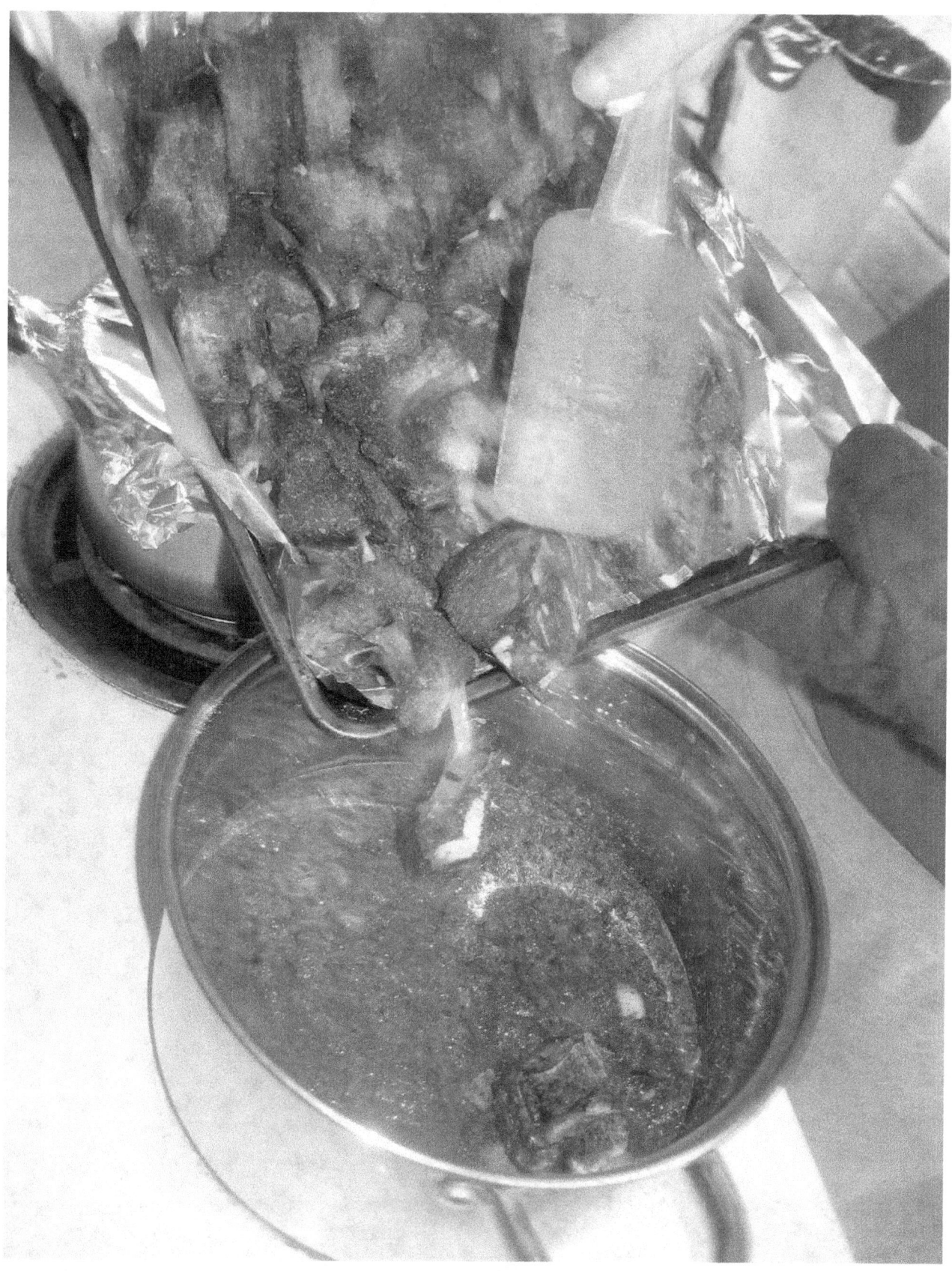

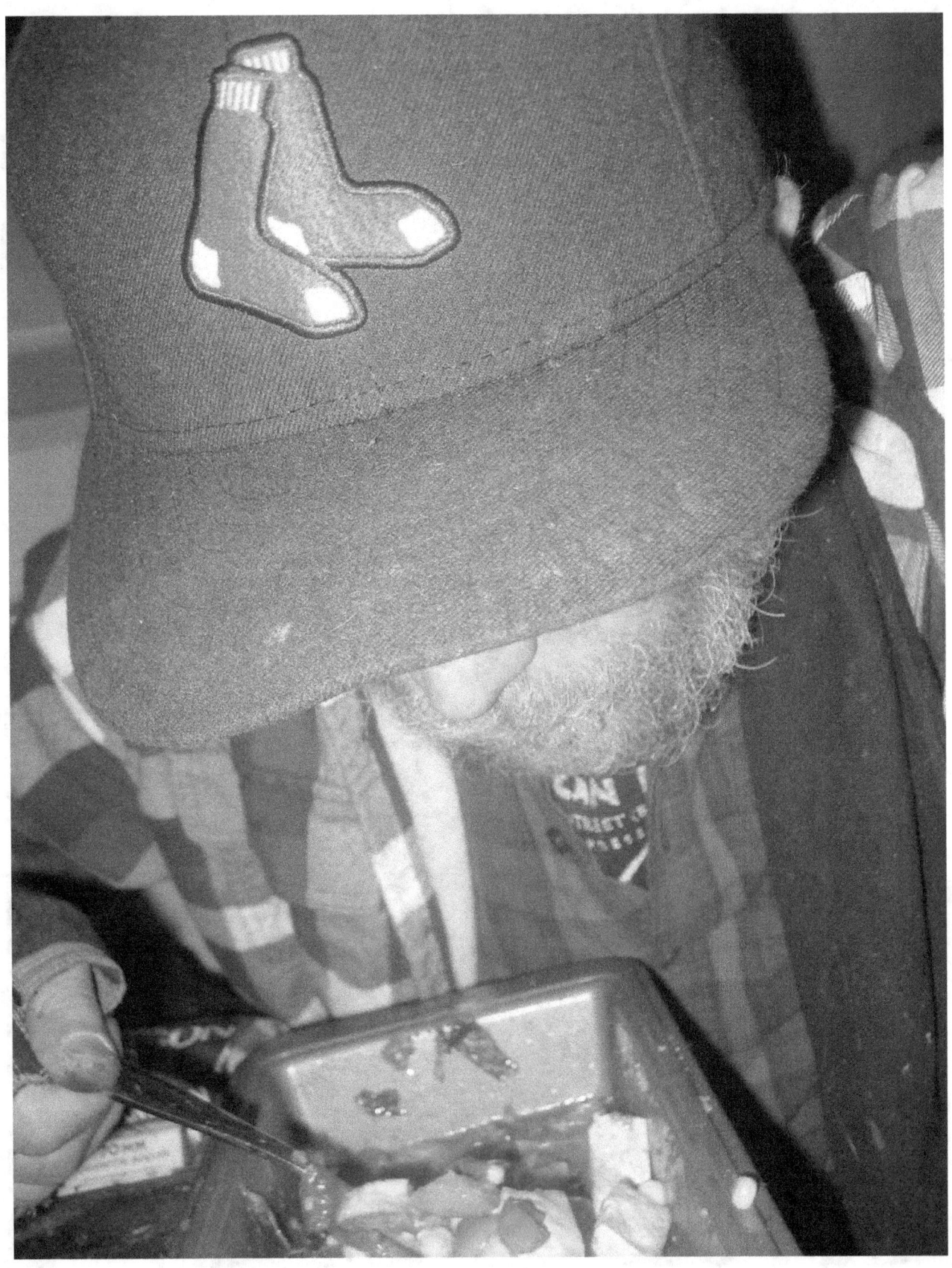

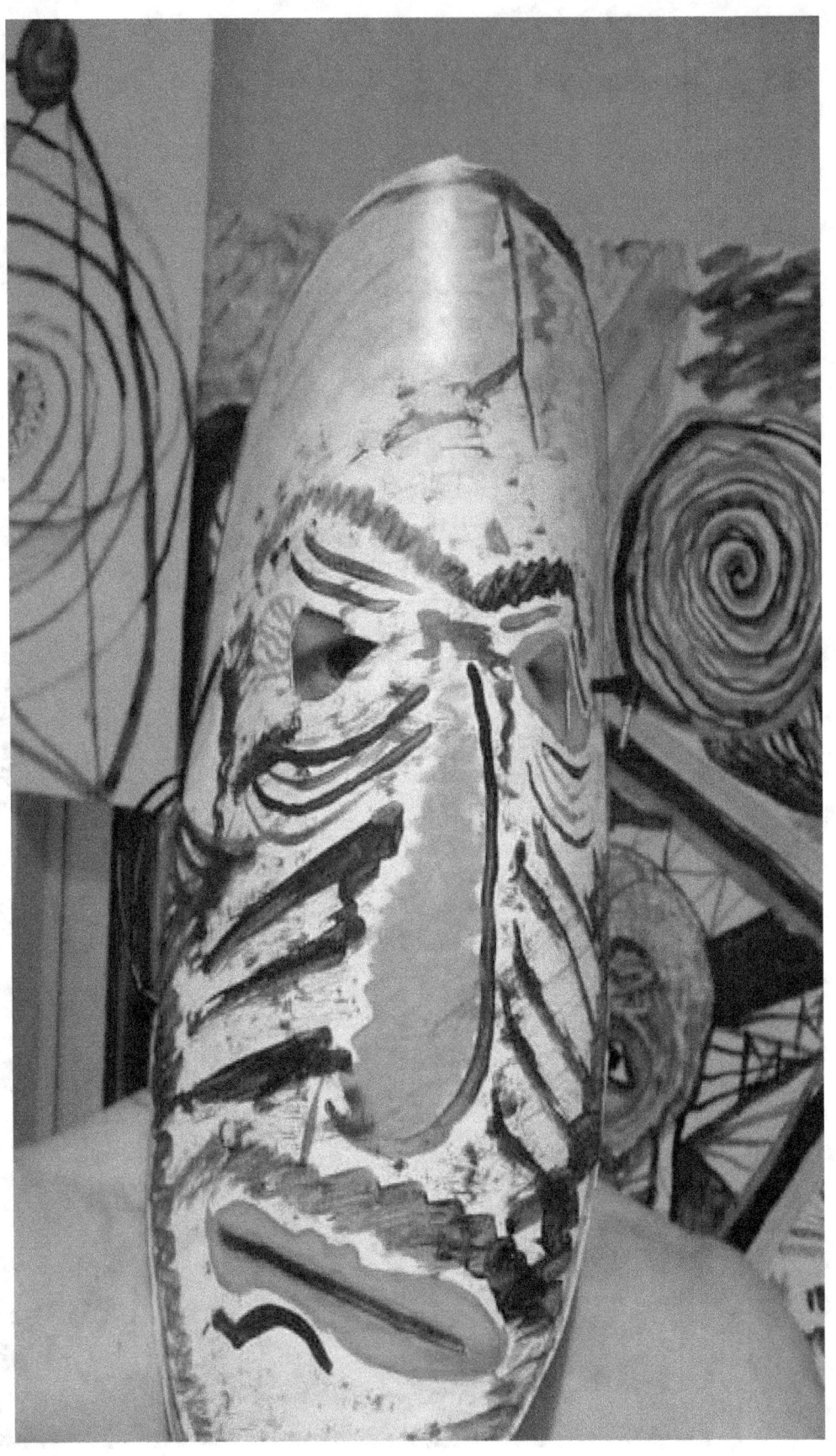

----------------------
Fin. June, 6 2018
Copies avail. @:

www.smileamazon.com
And, for reference:
www.shirleyanitajob.com

Teresamoon Big promotion watch Christmas Cheapest Woman Mens Quartz Wrist Watch (Brown) Price: $1.22 Shipping: $2.99 (China Post)

# Cool Men's 8MM Black Lava Stone Gold Lion Beaded Charm Bracelet Gift Cheapest

Princely Price: $2.97 Shipping: Free